How to Draw for Children and Young Adults
SUPERCHARACTERS

Earl R. Phelps

How To Draw For Children and Young Adults: Supercharacters

By Earl R. Phelps

Copyright © 2018 by Earl R. Phelps

All rights reserved. Any reproduction or other unauthorized use of the material or artwork herein is prohibited without the express written permission of the author.

Published by Phelps Publishing
P.O. Box 22401
Cleveland, Ohio 44122

ISBN: 978-1-887627-10-8
Library of Congress Control Number: 2018900162

Printed in the United States of American

Visit our website at www.phelpspublishing.com

Table of Contents

Introduction	4
4 Eye Man	5
Back Cape Hero	9
Bubble Man	13
Bubble Man Back	17
Cubic Man	21
Egg Man	25
Fly Man	29
X-Ray Lady	33
Lady Hero	37
Afro Lady	41
Man Crash Wood	45
Melting Head	49
Saturn Man	53
Steel Man	57
Oval Queen	61

Introduction

Hello,

What's going on?

I appreciate your interest in my book. I created this book not only with the purpose of teaching you how to draw, but to enjoy yourself while doing it. That's what it's all about, having fun.

All you need is a pencil and paper to start drawing. I drew everything in this book free hand, using only pencils. I did not use any type of rulers or circles for my drawings, but you can if you choose to.

You can learn how to draw your own supercharacters with these simple step-by-step illustrations. Anyone can learn from this book, from ages 8 to 108. It's all about just putting together circles, squares and lines.

This book is so simple that the illustrations alone will guide you through everything. No words are needed to explain. As the saying goes "A picture is worth a thousand words. "

The key to success is to practice, practice and more practice.

Enjoy yourself and let's get Busy!!

Earl R. Phelps

4 Eye Man

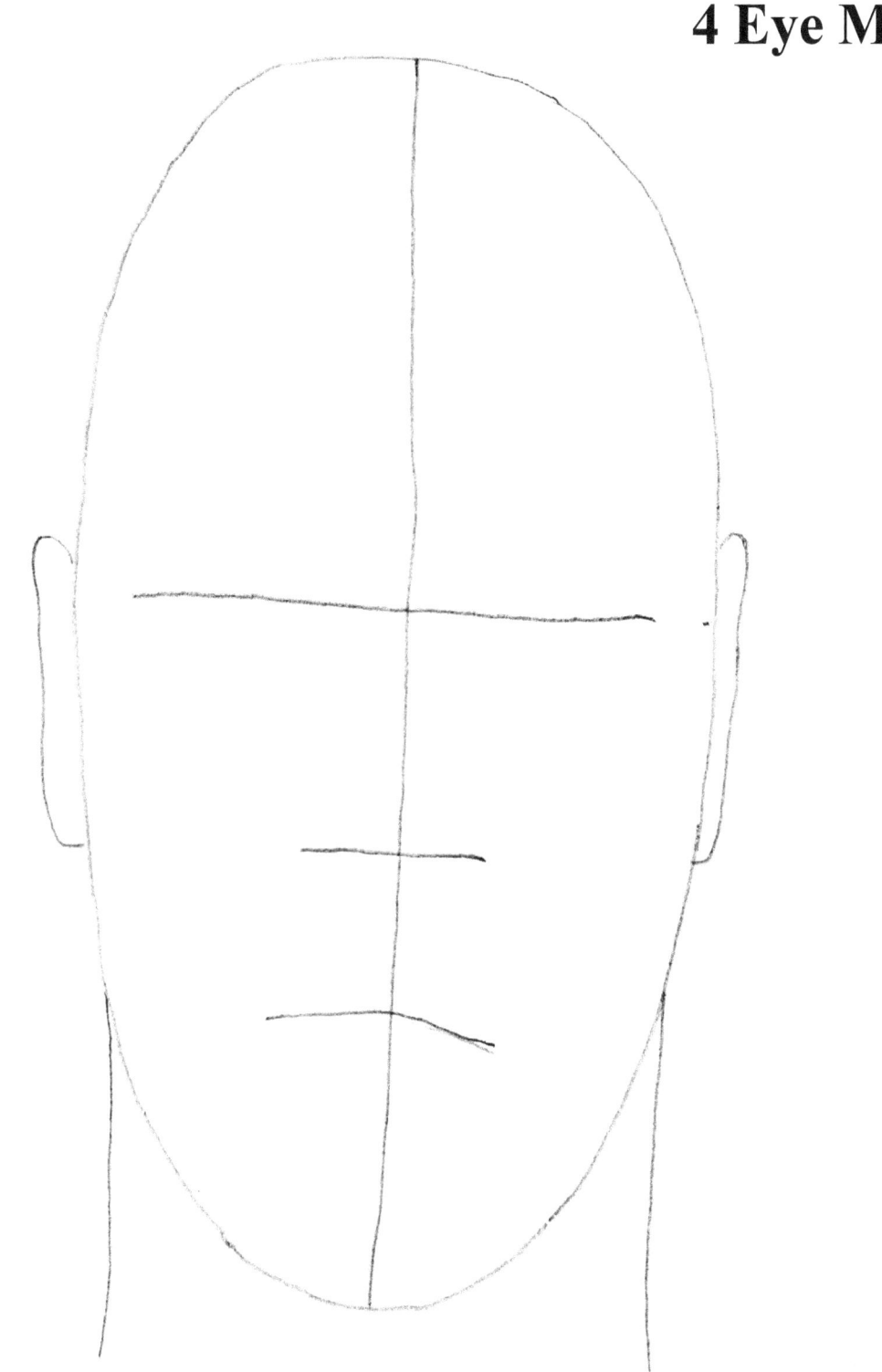

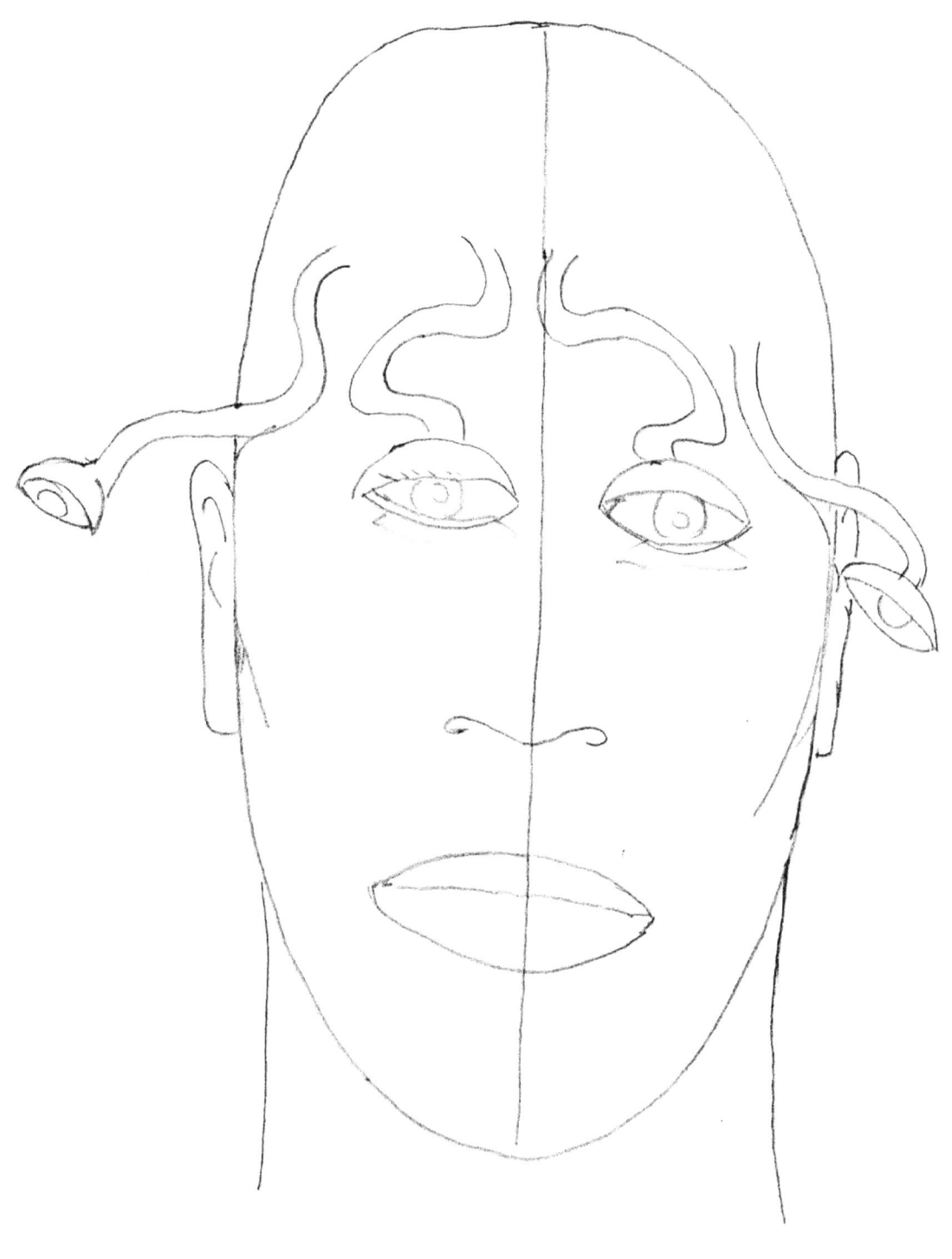

Back Cape Hero

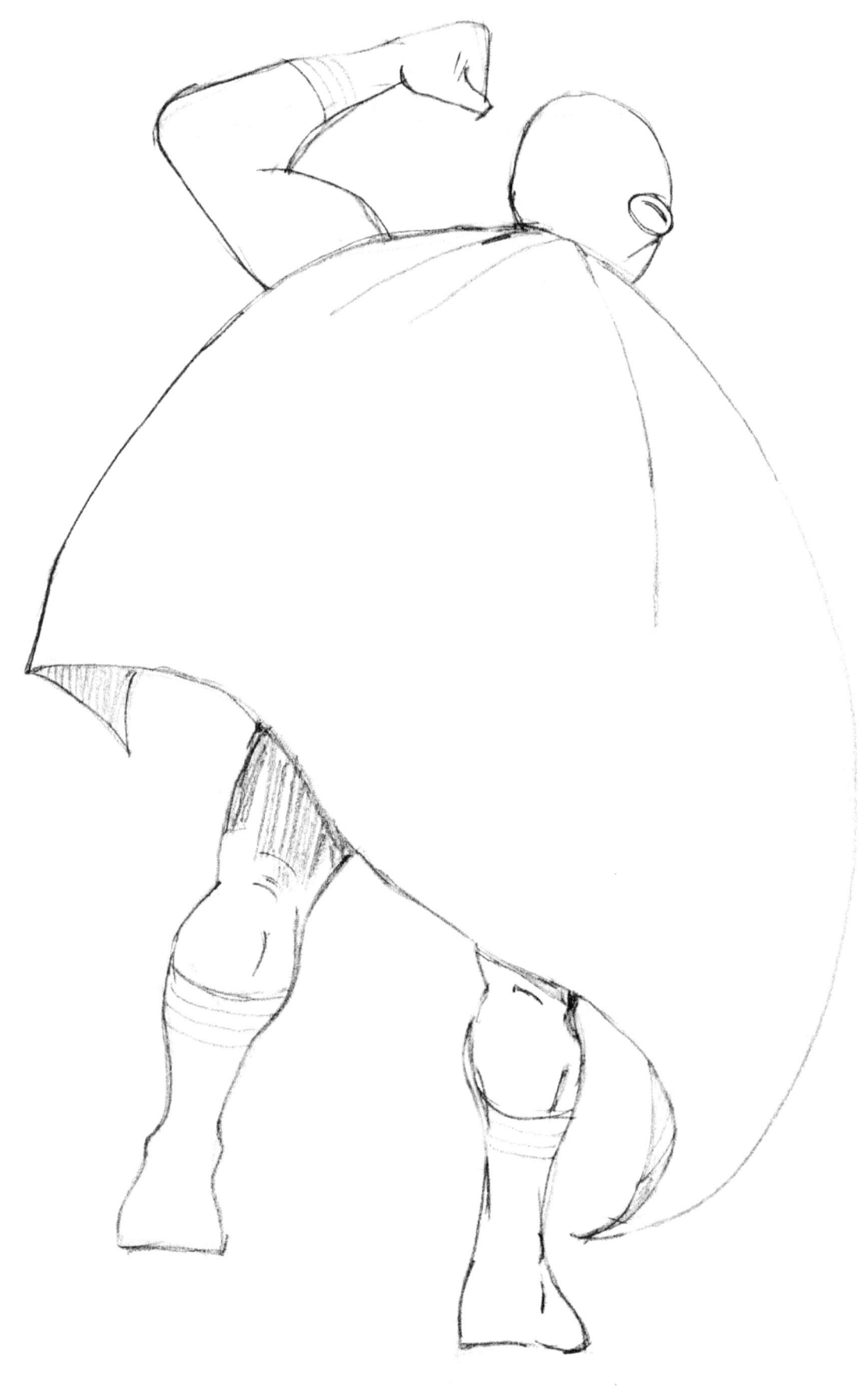

Bubble Man

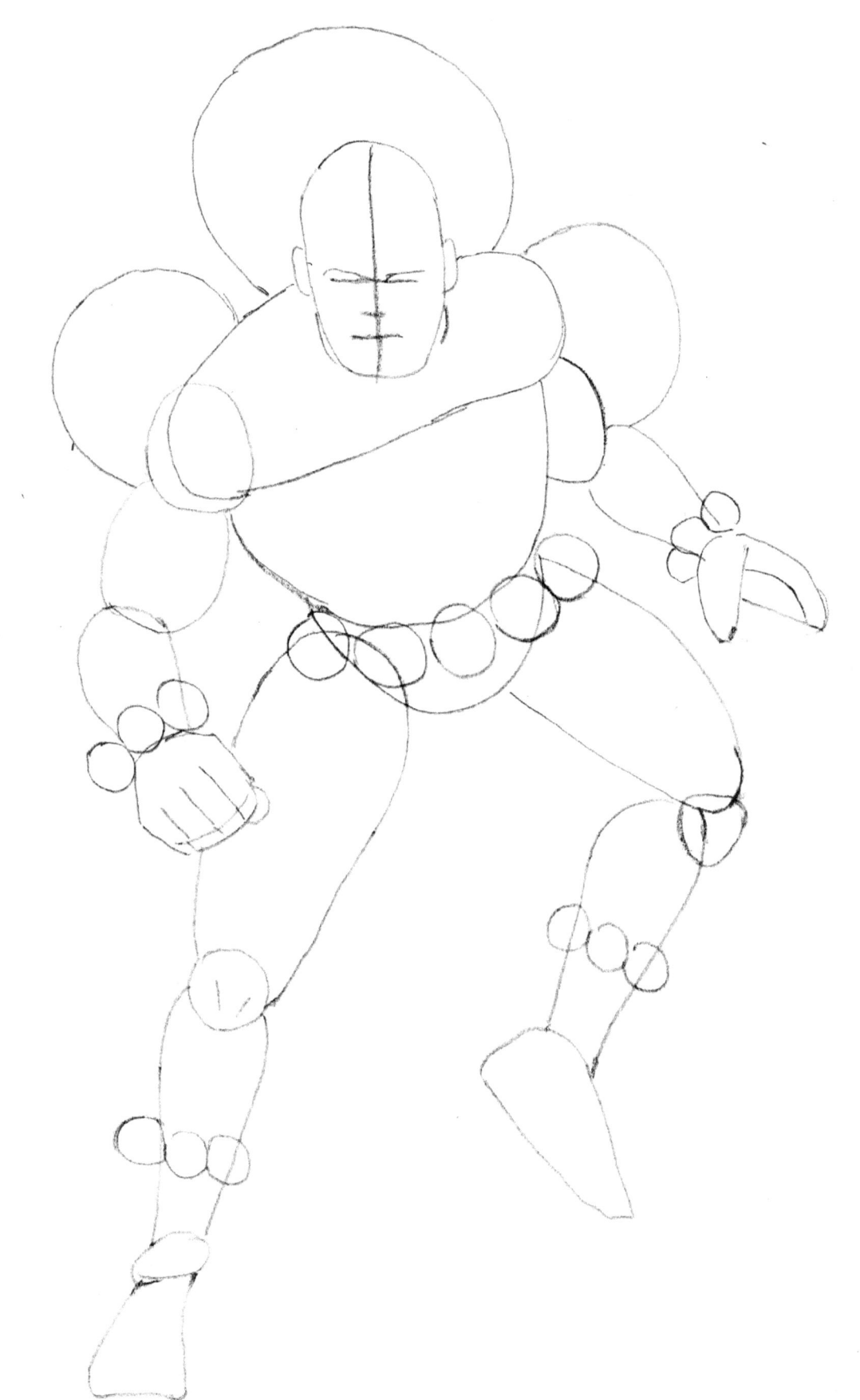

Bubble Man Back

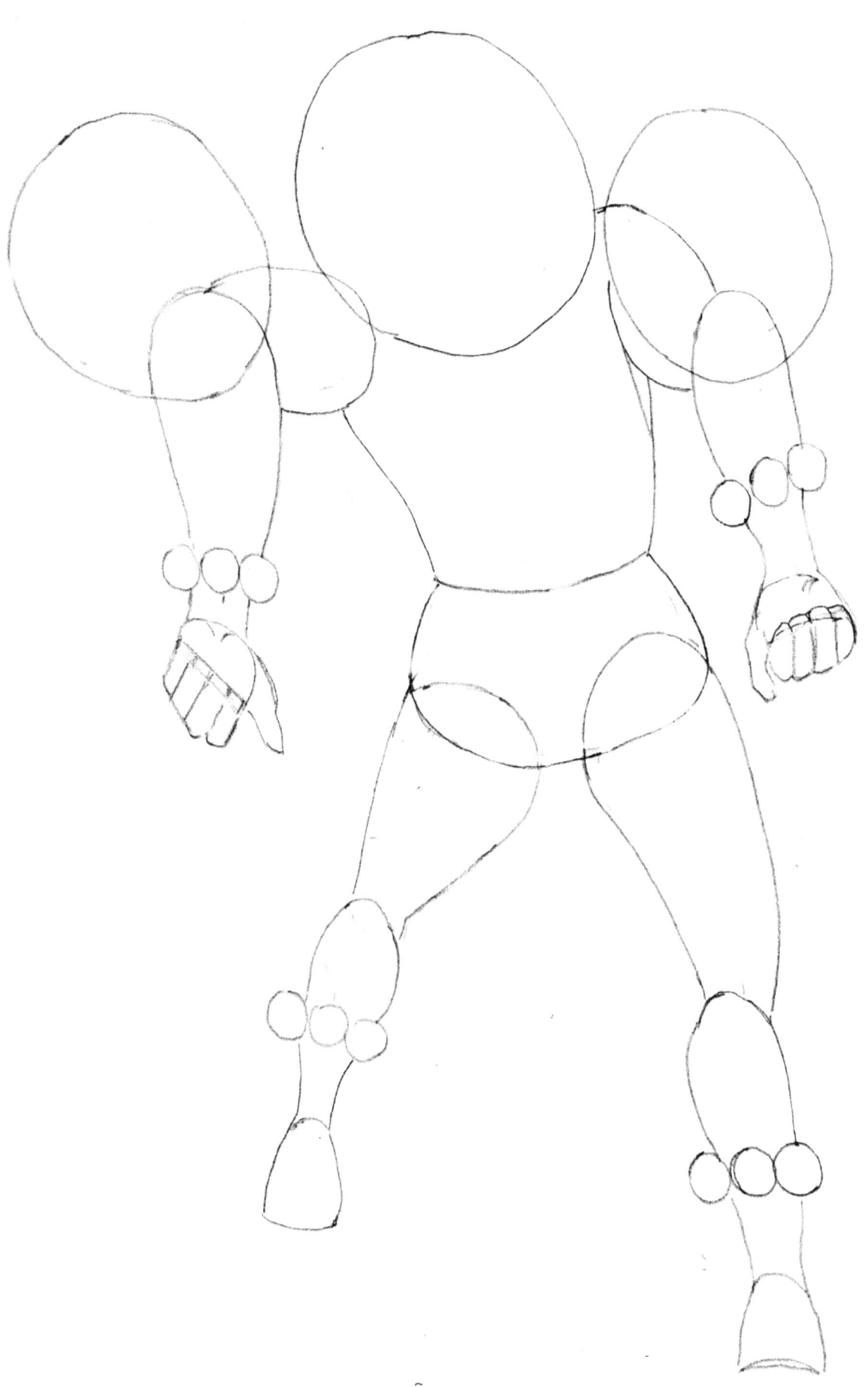

Cubic Man

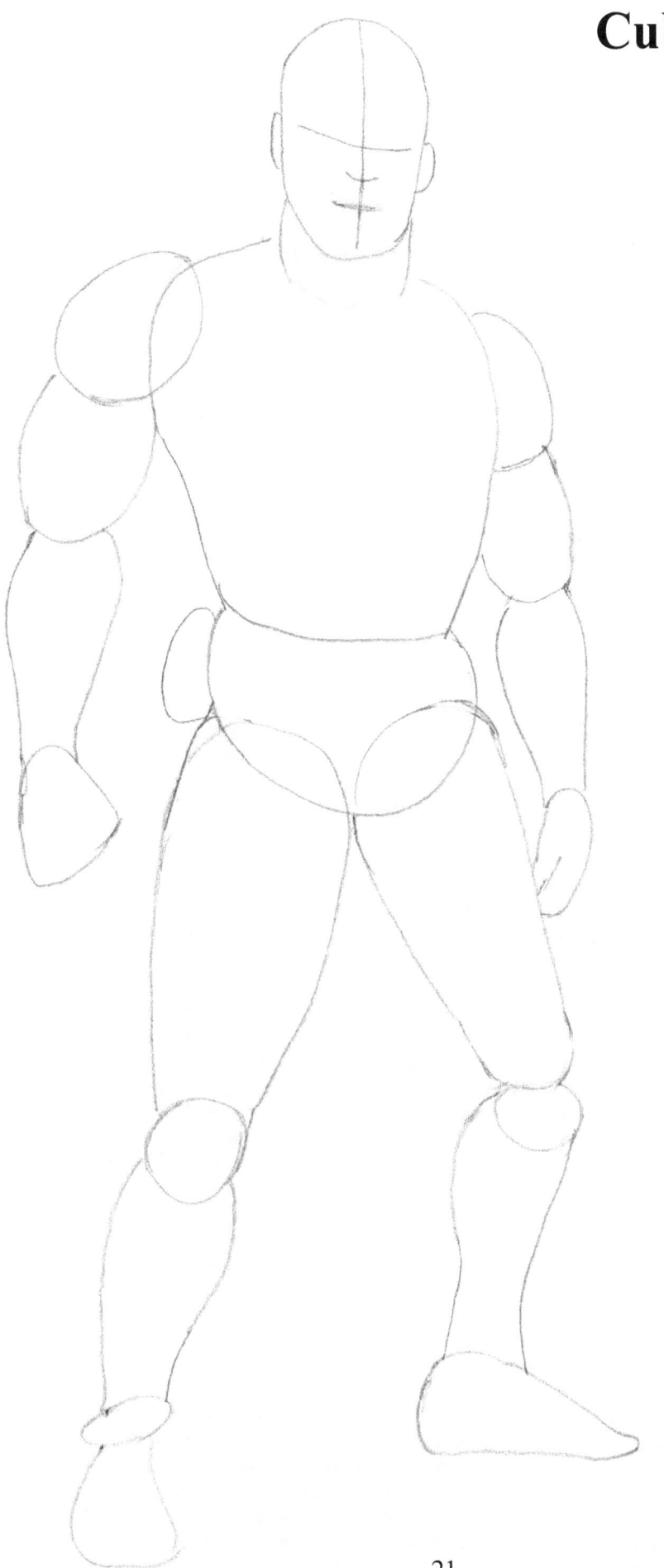

Egg Man

Fly Man

X-Ray Lady

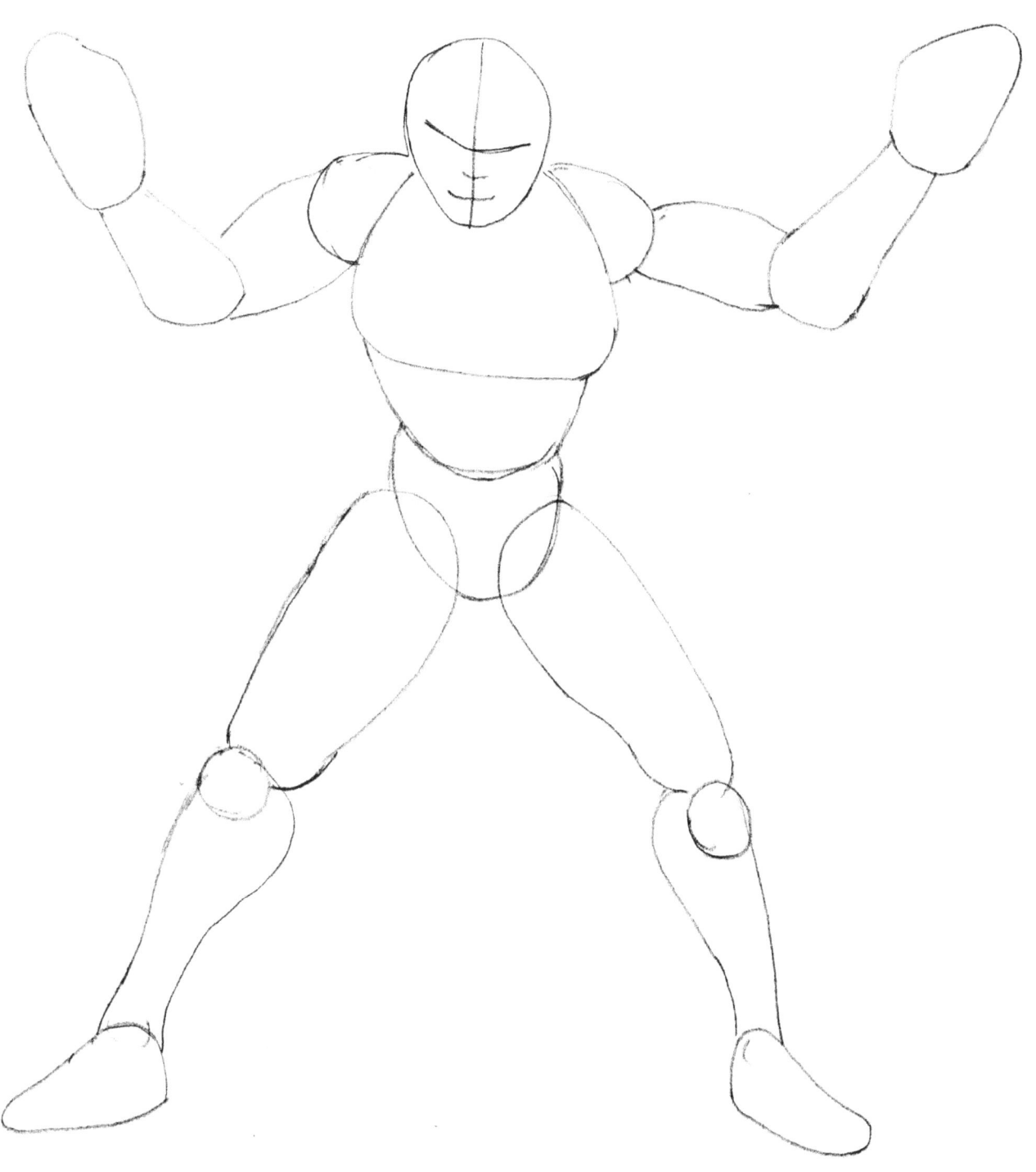

Lady Hero

Afro Lady

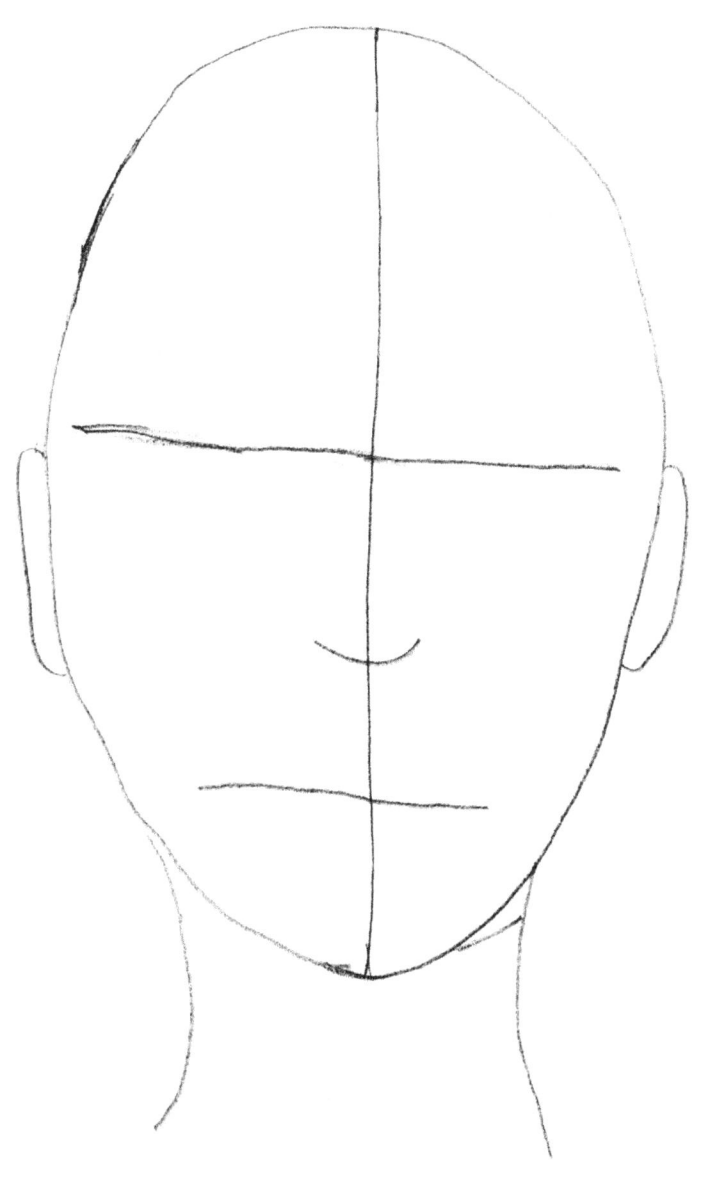

Hero Crash Wood

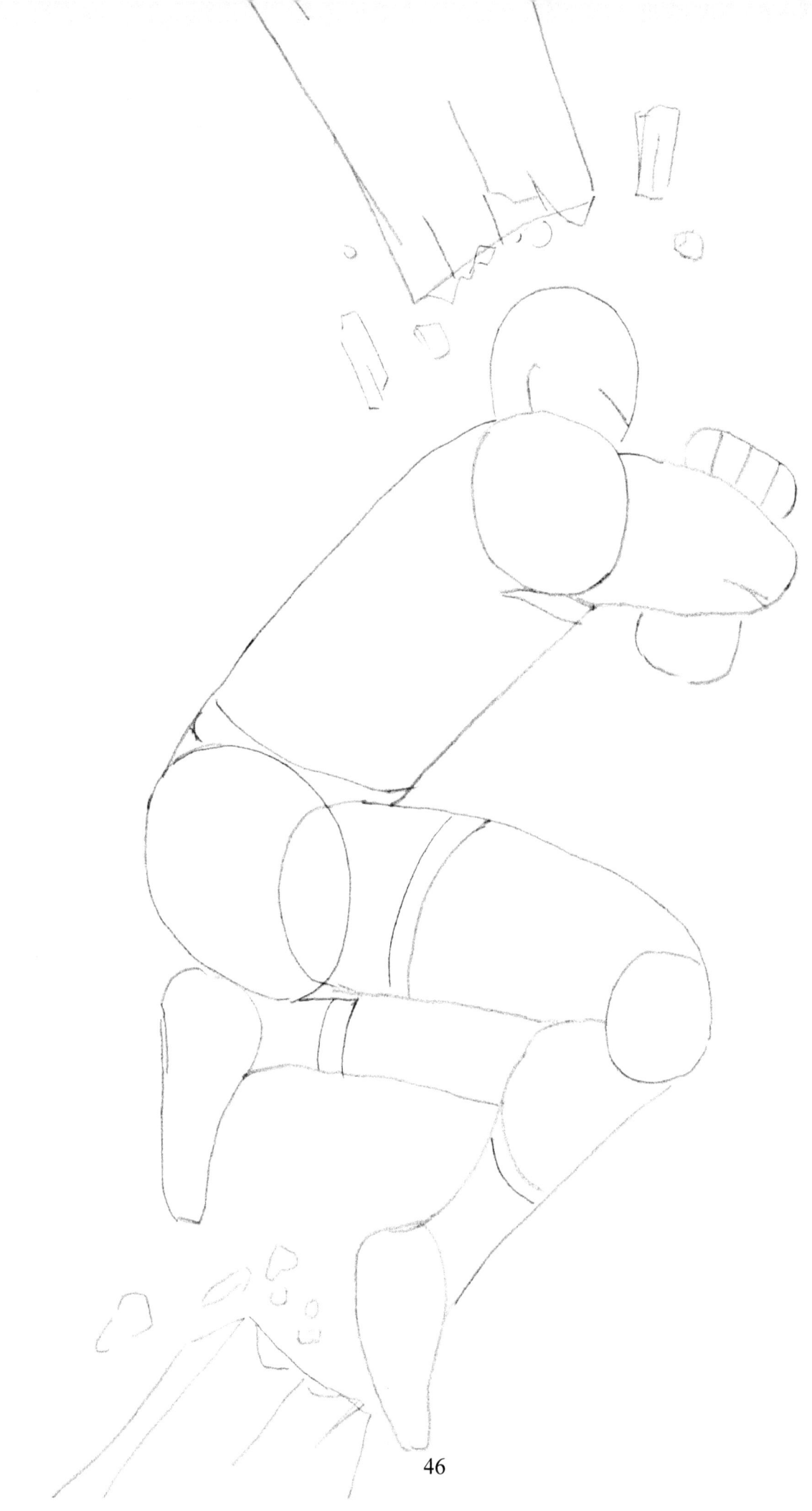

Melting Man

49

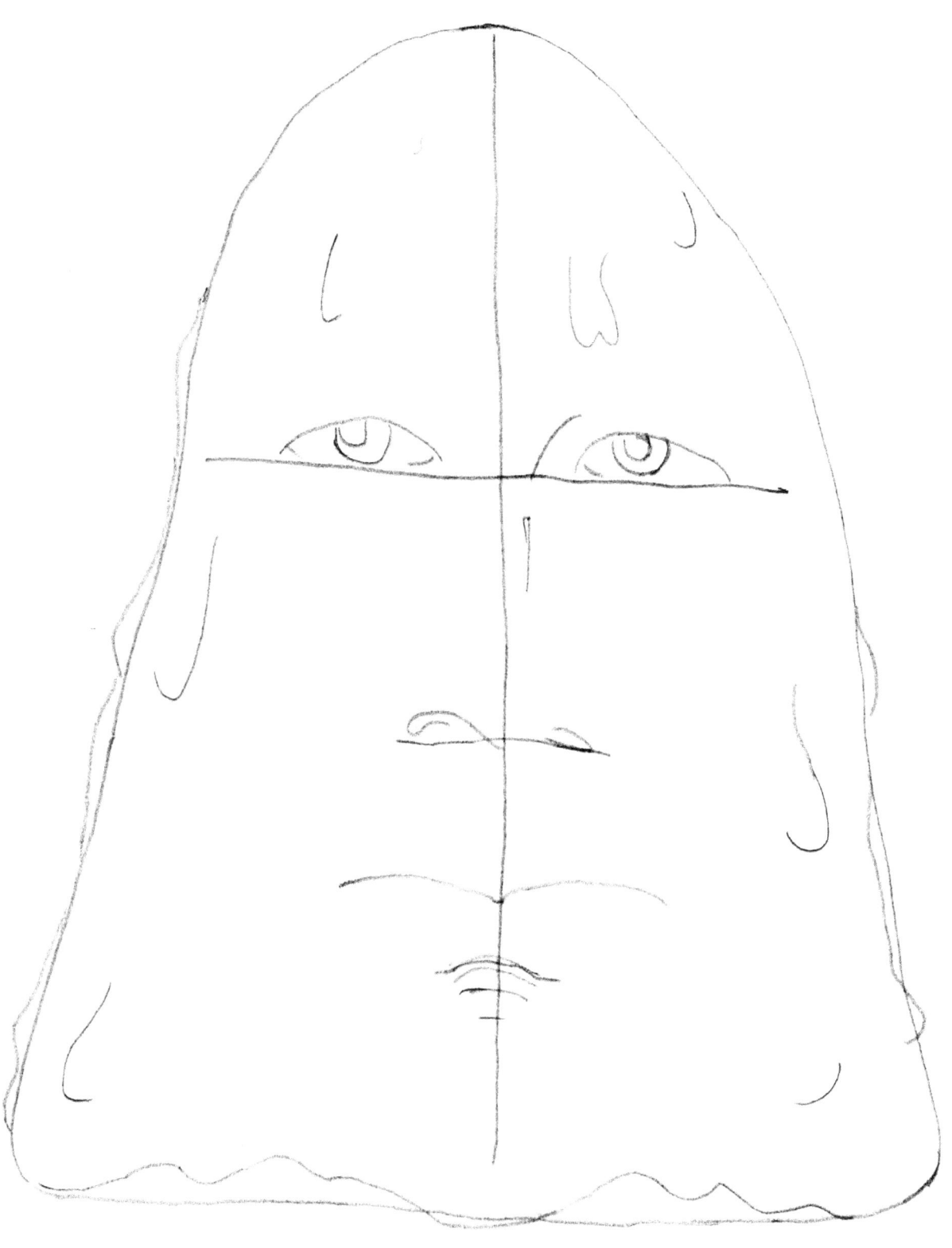

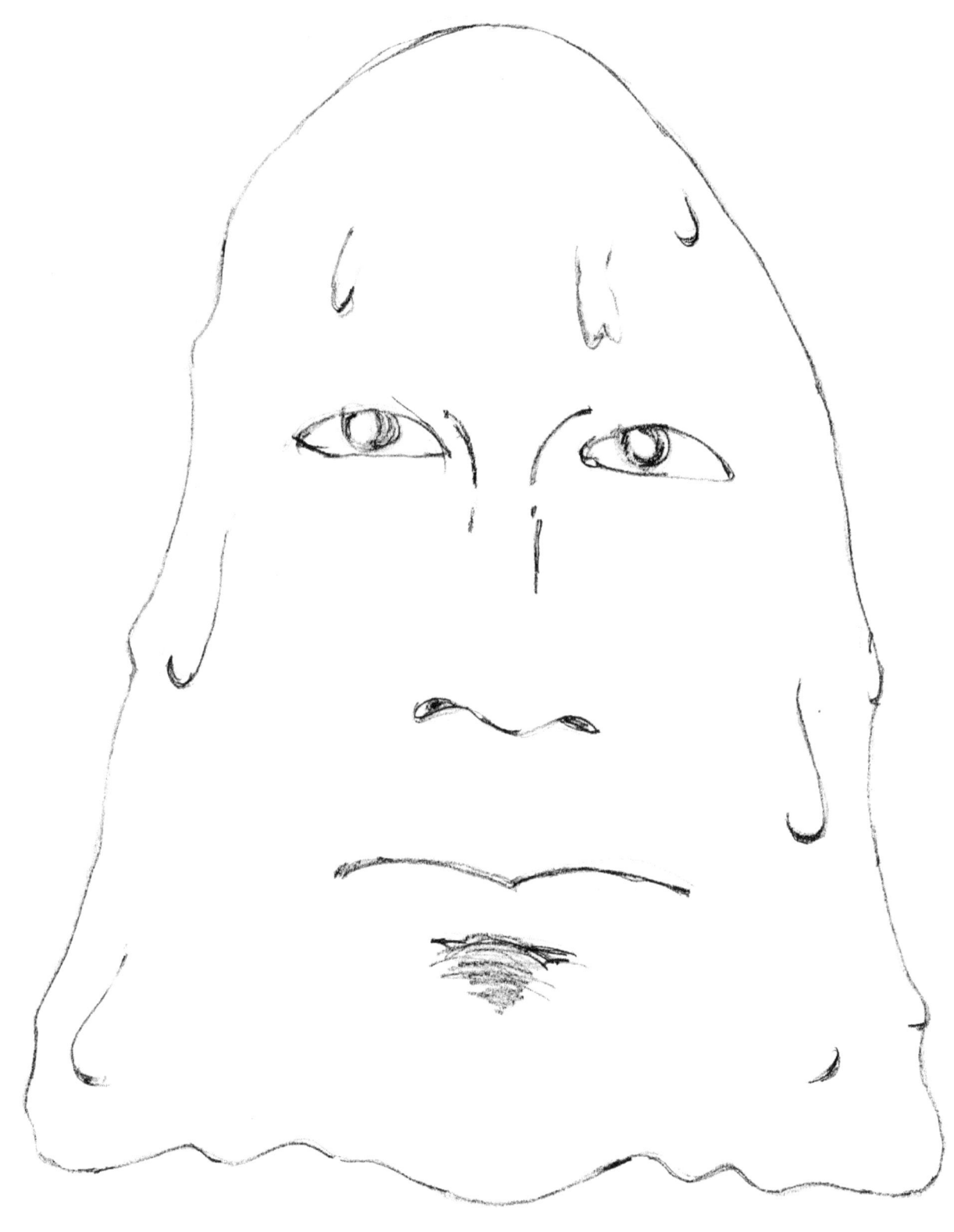

Saturn Man

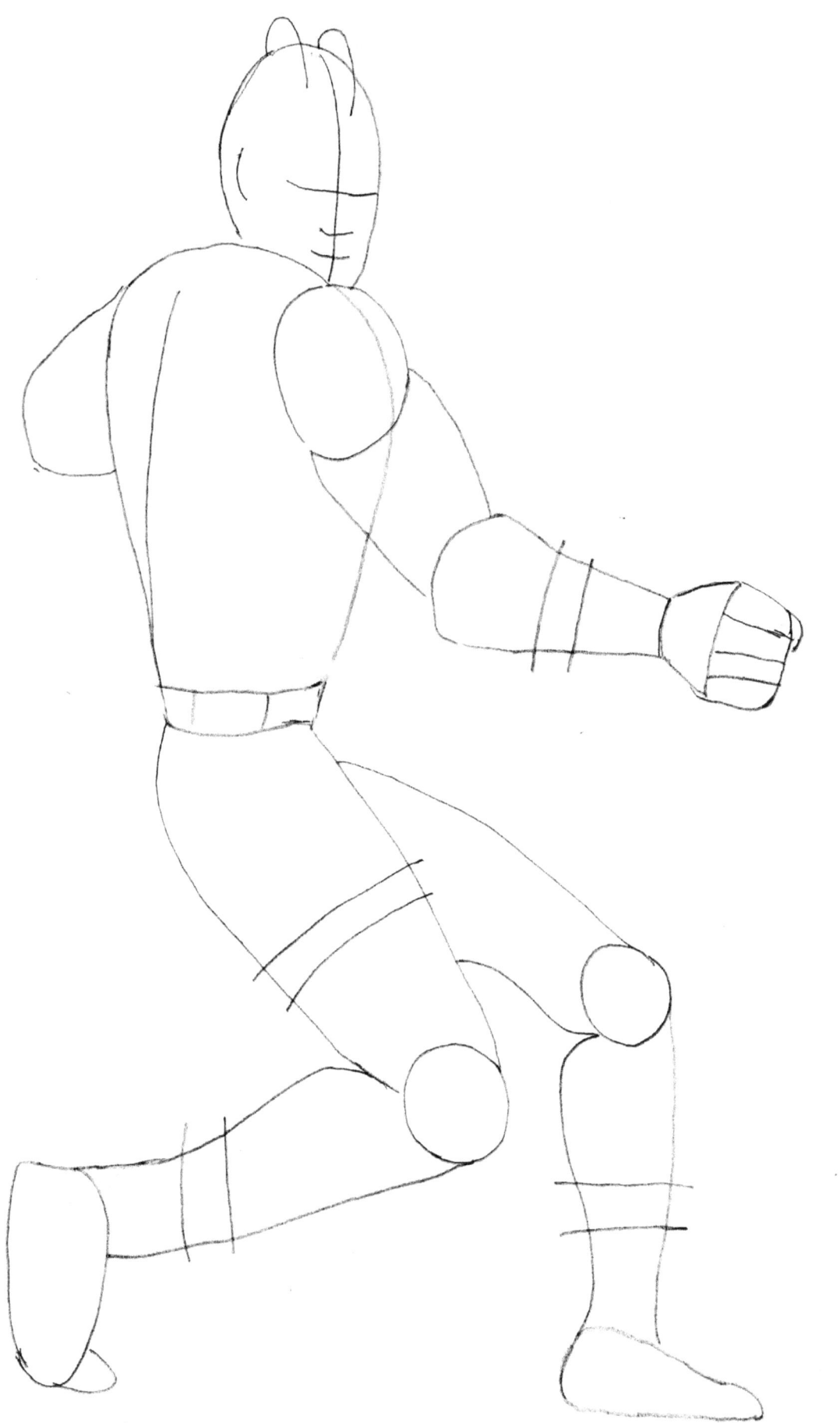

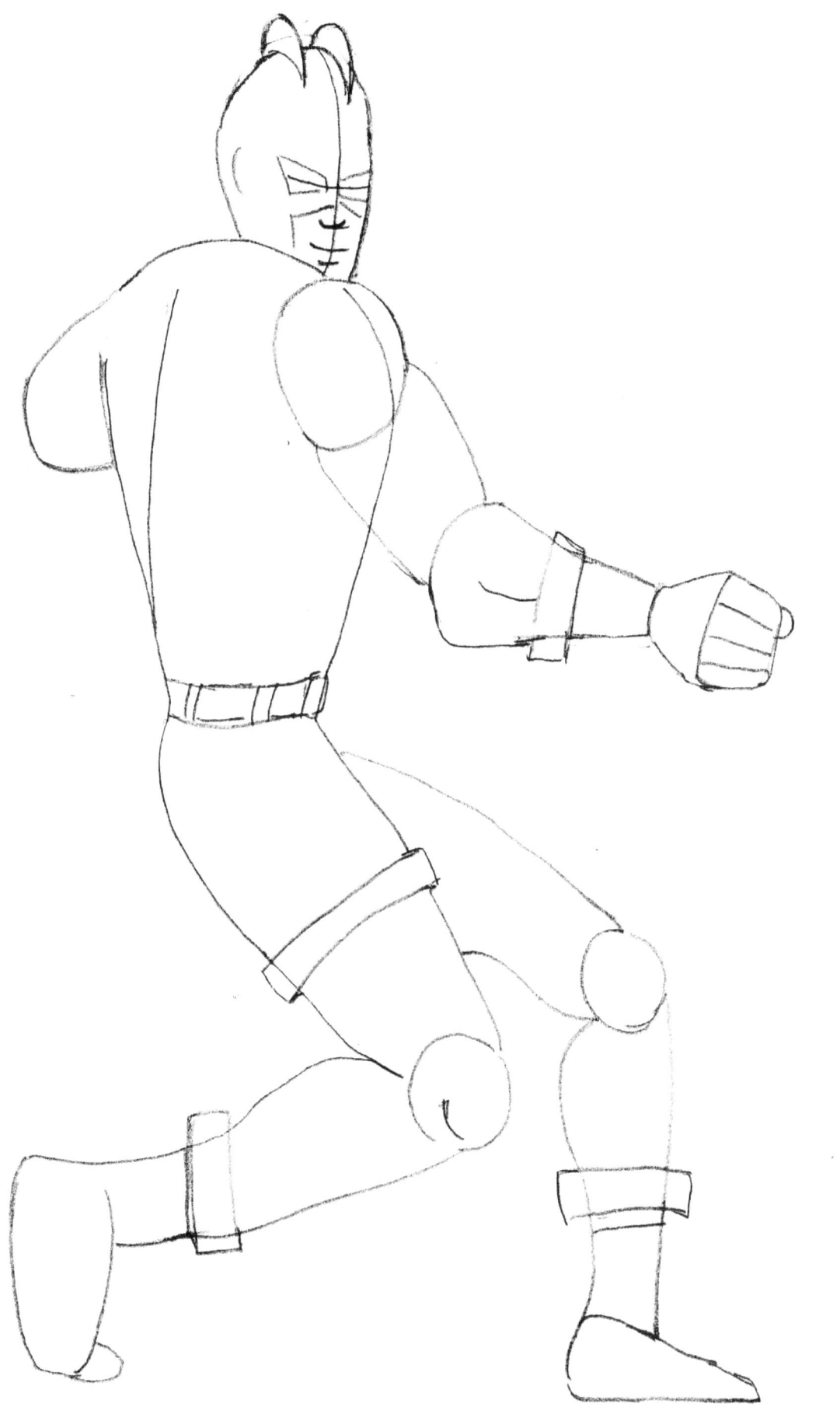

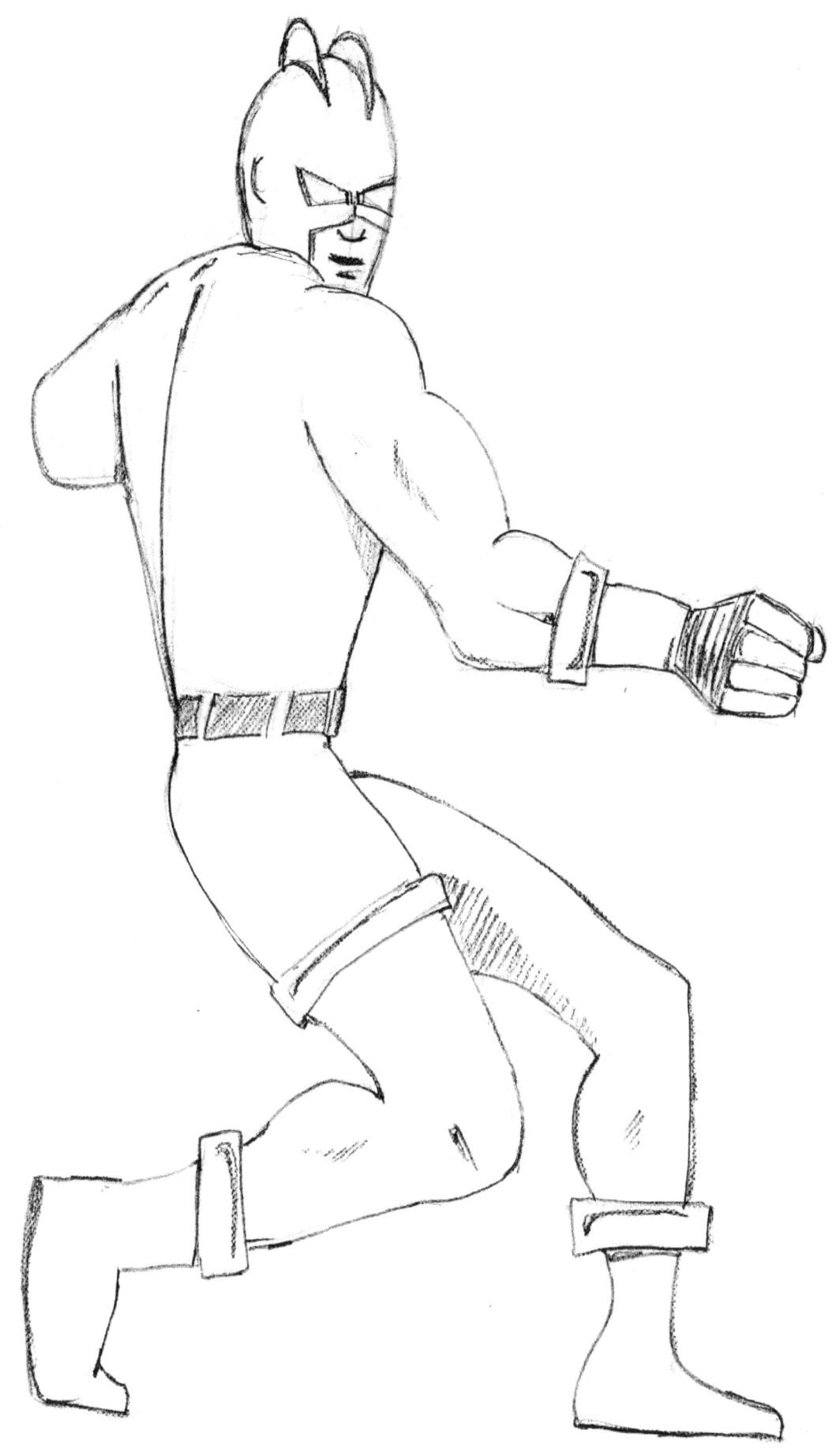

Steel Man

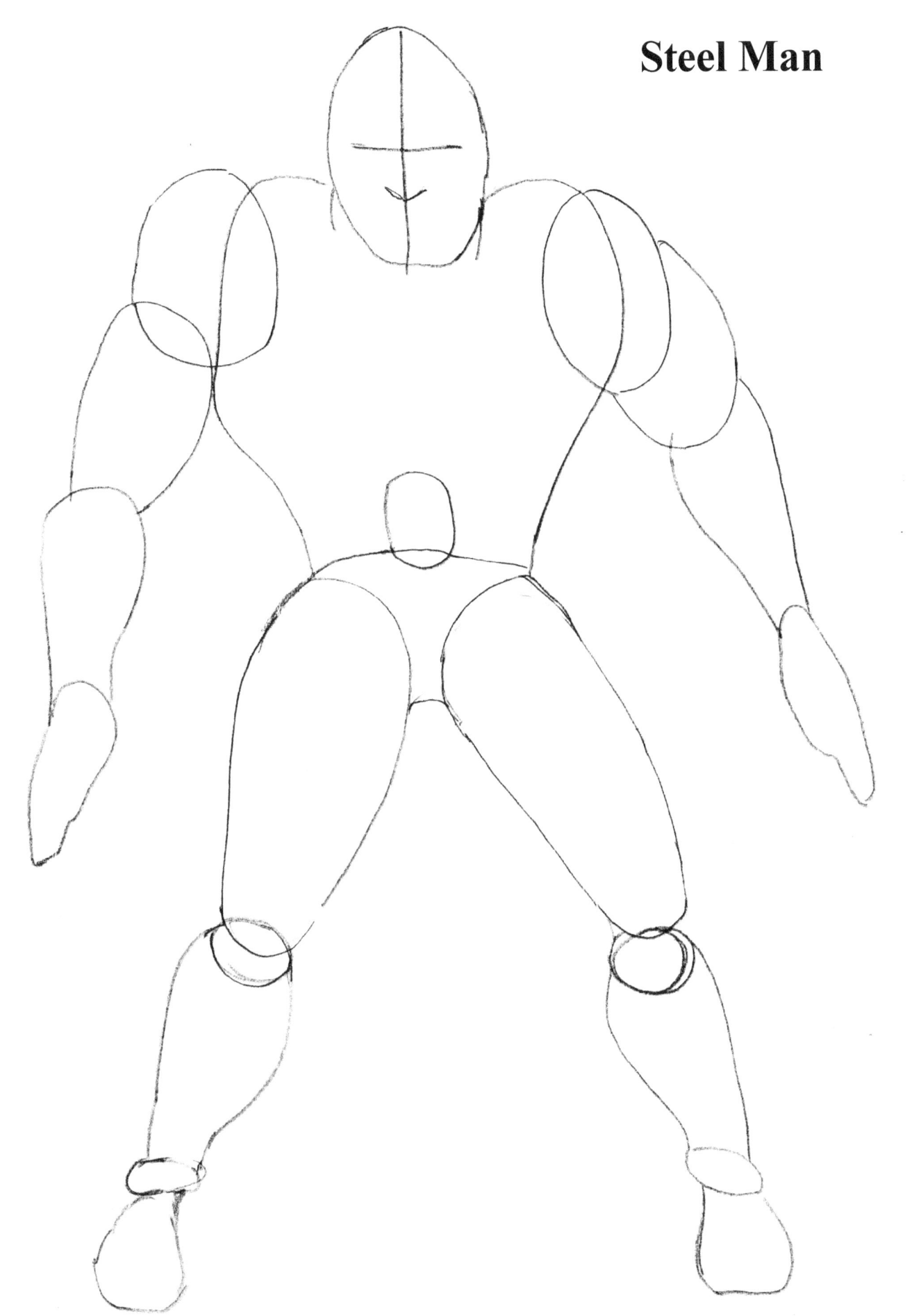

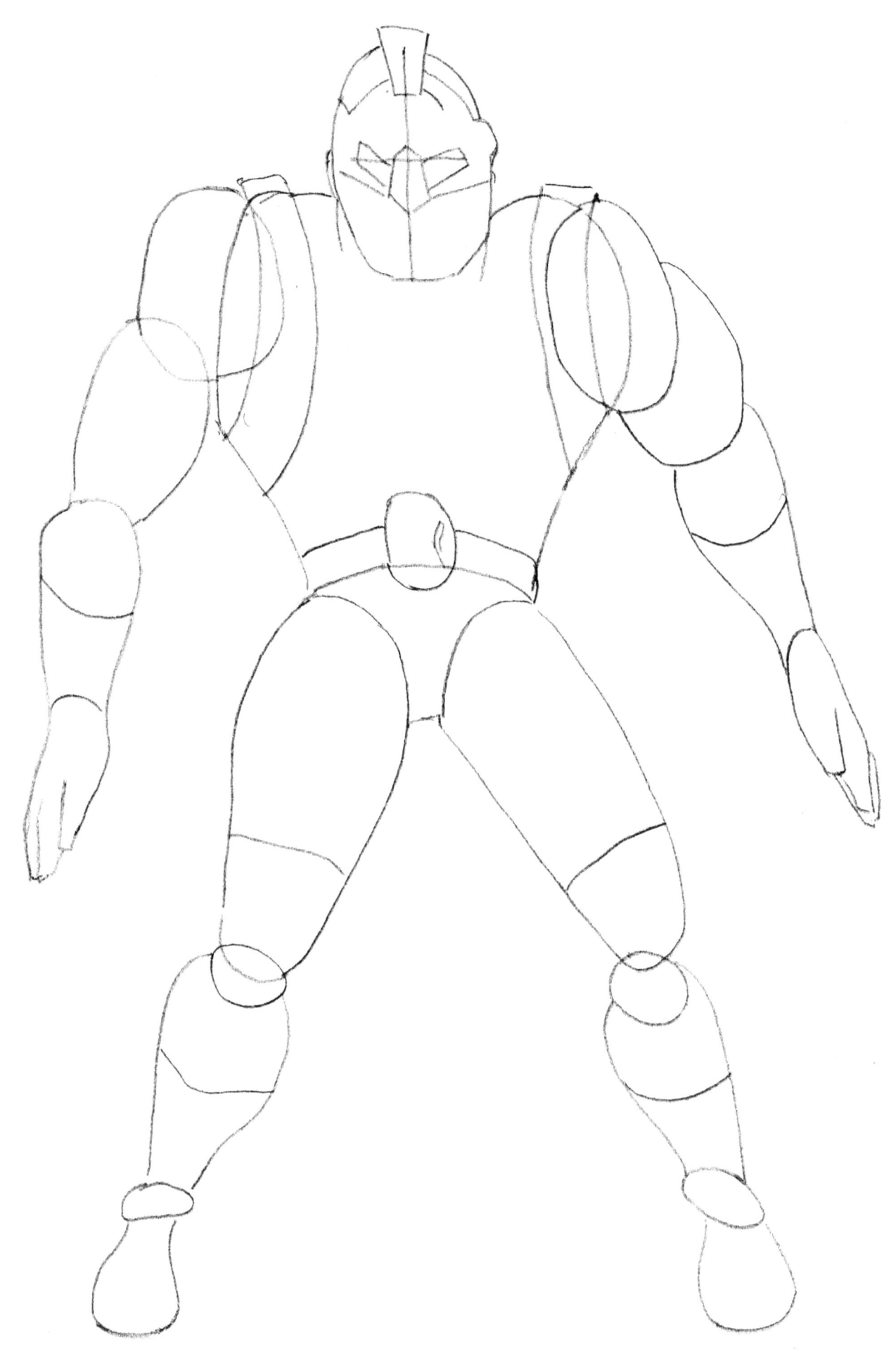

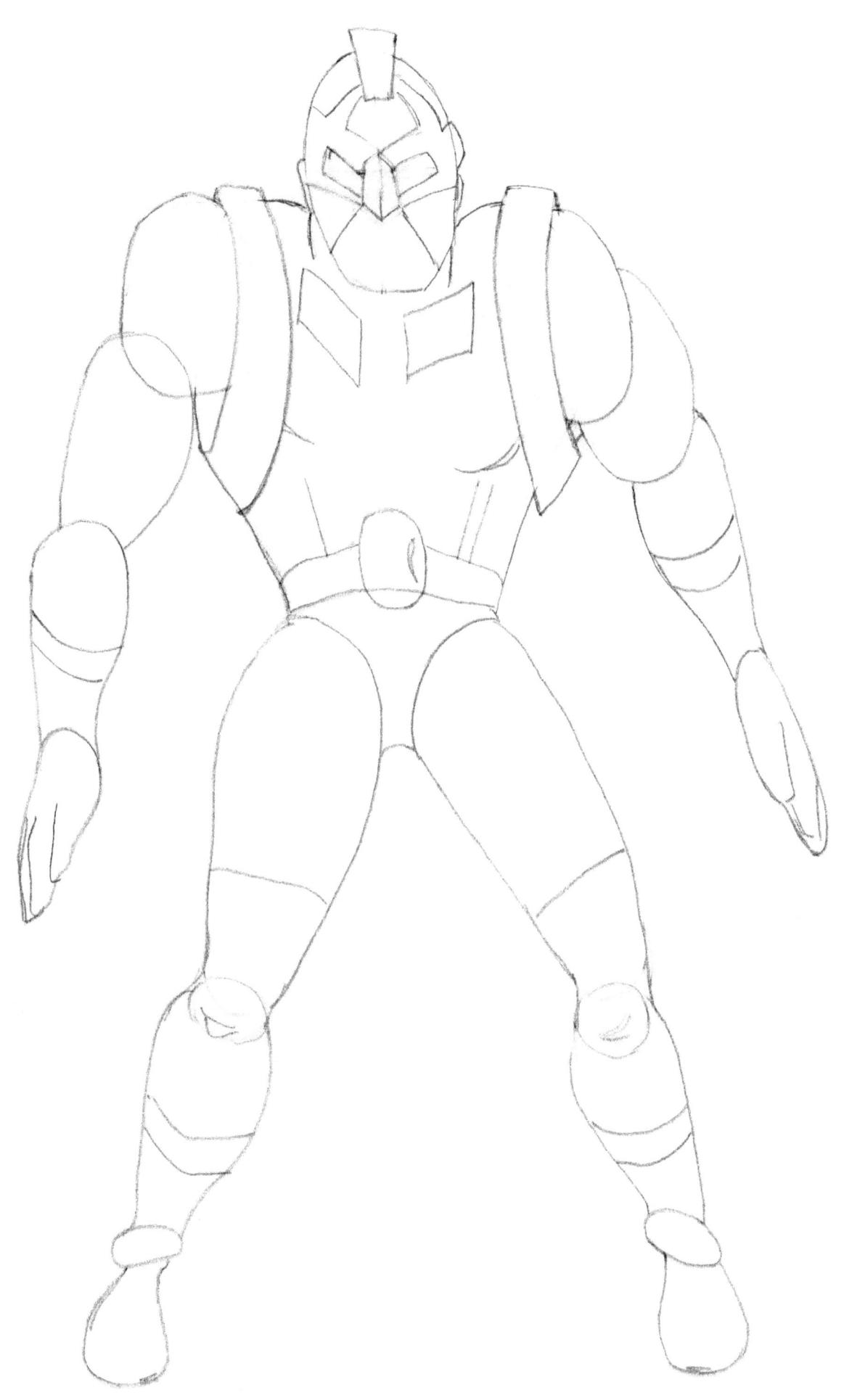

Oval Queen

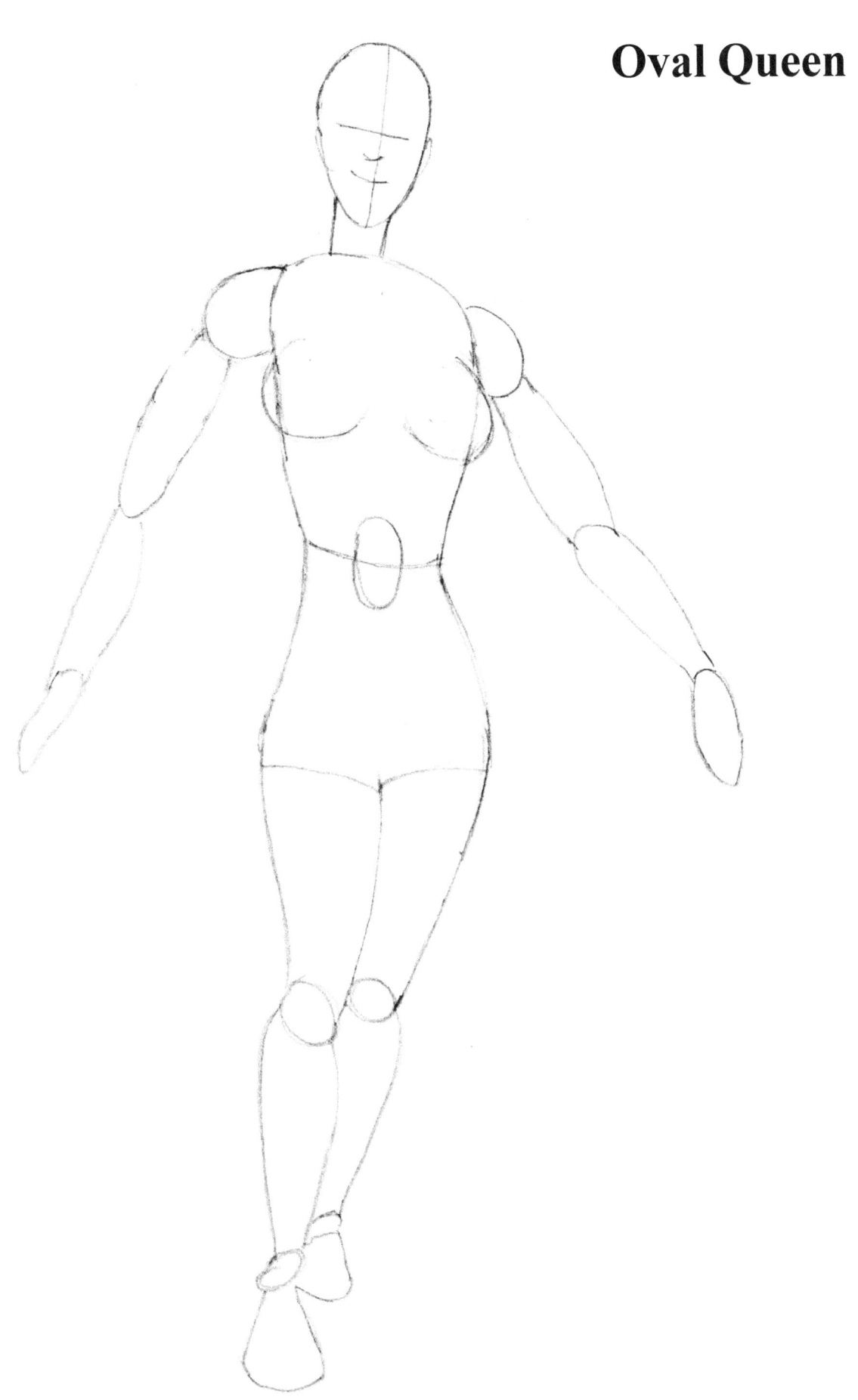

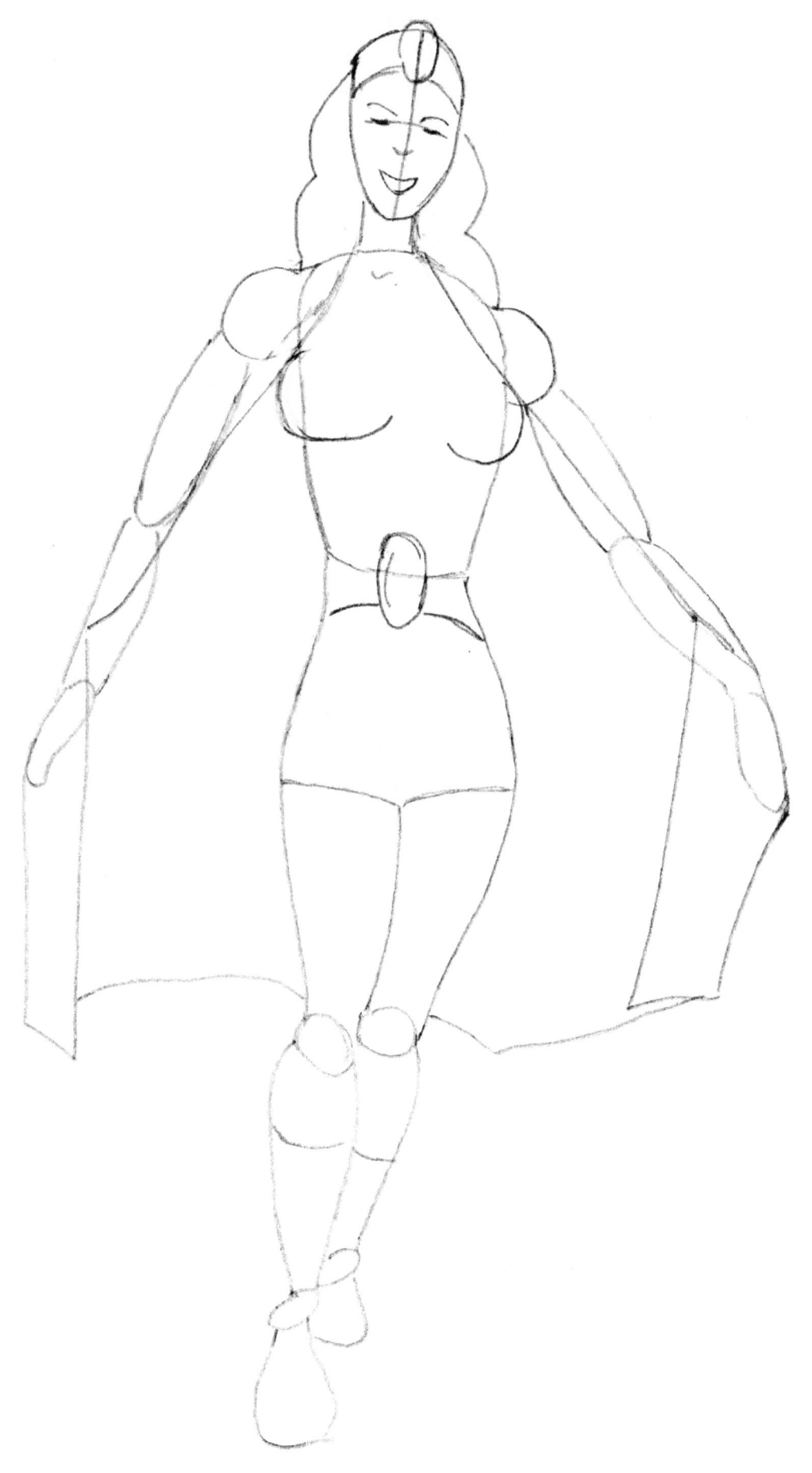